# OSV Kids The Rosary

# The Rosary

Colleen Pressprich
Illustrated by Steliyana Doneva

OSV Kids
Huntington, Indiana

*Nihil Obstat*
Msgr. Michael Heintz, Ph.D.
*Censor Librorum*

*Imprimatur*
✠ Kevin C. Rhoades
Bishop of Fort Wayne-South Bend
January 21, 2025

The *Nihil Obstat* and *Imprimatur* are official declarations that a book is free from doctrinal or moral error. It is not implied that those who have granted the *Nihil Obstat* and *Imprimatur* agree with the contents, opinions, or statements expressed.



30 29 28 27 26 25     1 2 3 4 5 6 7 8 9



Our Sunday Visitor Publishing Division
Our Sunday Visitor, Inc.
200 Noll Plaza
Huntington, IN 46750
www.osv.com
1-800-348-2440

ISBN: 978-1-63966-373-6 (Inventory No. T3002)

1. JUVENILE NONFICTION—Religious—Christian—Devotional & Prayer.
2. RELIGION—Christian Ritual & Practice—General
3. RELIGION—Christianity—Catholic.

LCCN: 2025935650

Cover and interior design: Lindsey Riesen
Cover and interior art: Steliyana Doneva

PRINTED IN THE UNITED STATES OF AMERICA

*For Levi and Gwen with love from Aunt Colleen*

*The Rosary is the most beautiful and the most rich in graces of all prayers; it is the prayer that touches most the Heart of the Mother of God.*

— Pope Saint Pius X

# Introduction

The Rosary is a traditional Catholic prayer. It has been prayed by Catholics all over the world for centuries. It is beautiful, powerful, and only takes about 20 minutes to pray!

Here's how the Rosary works.

When we pray a Rosary, we repeat a set of prayers five times. Each repetition is called a decade because of the ten Hail Marys it includes. The word "decade" comes from the Latin word *decem*, which means "ten." With each decade, we meditate on (which means think and pray about) an important moment in the life of Jesus or Mary while we pray. These important moments are called the Mysteries of the Rosary. They are organized into four groups: the Joyful Mysteries, the Luminous Mysteries, the Sorrowful Mysteries, and the Glorious Mysteries. Each set of mysteries is assigned a day (or days) of the week.

While praying the Rosary, we use a set of beads to keep track of where we are in the prayers. But you can still pray the Rosary if you don't have rosary beads with you! You can keep count in your head or even use your fingers.

Often when people pray the Rosary, they do it for a particular intention. An intention is something or someone that we are praying for. You can offer the whole Rosary for a single intention or choose a different person or request for each decade.

# How to Pray the Rosary

1. Holding the crucifix, make the **Sign of the Cross**. Then pray the **Apostles' Creed**.

2. On the first large bead, pray an **Our Father**.

3. On the next three beads pray the **Hail Mary** for faith, hope, and love. Finish with a **Glory Be**.

4. At the large bead, read the meditation for the first mystery and pray an **Our Father**.

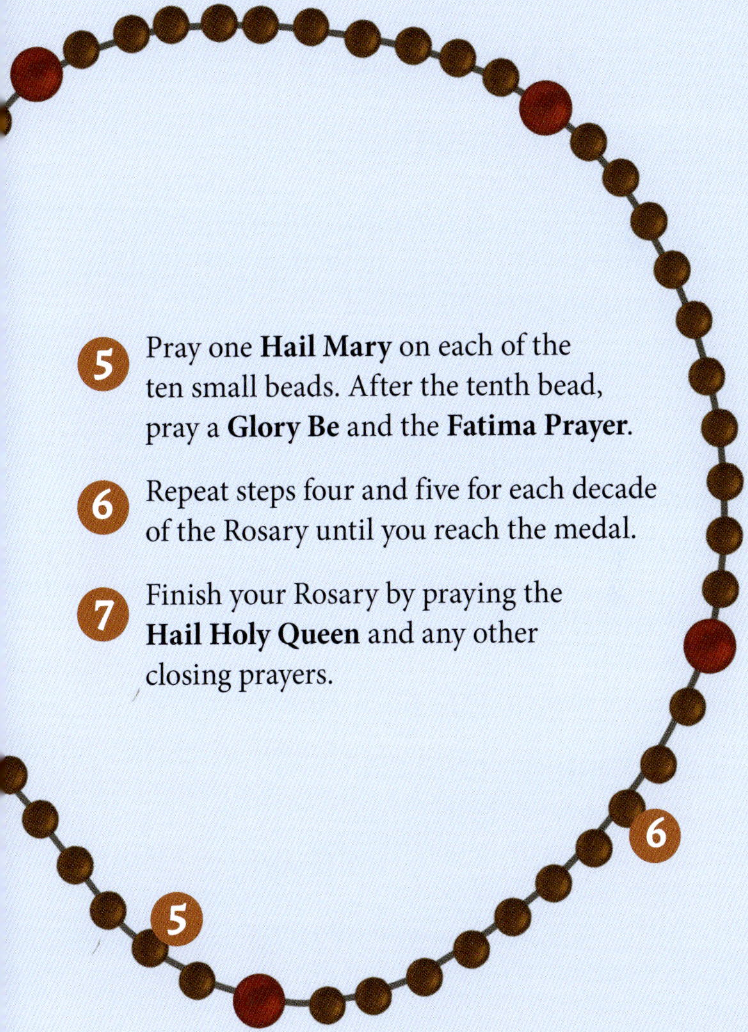


5. Pray one **Hail Mary** on each of the ten small beads. After the tenth bead, pray a **Glory Be** and the **Fatima Prayer**.

6. Repeat steps four and five for each decade of the Rosary until you reach the medal.

7. Finish your Rosary by praying the **Hail Holy Queen** and any other closing prayers.

# Prayers of the Rosary

## THE APOSTLES' CREED

I believe in God, the Father almighty, Creator of heaven and earth, and in Jesus Christ, his only Son, our Lord, who was conceived by the Holy Spirit, born of the Virgin Mary, suffered under Pontius Pilate, was crucified, died and was buried; he descended into hell;

on the third day he rose again from the dead; he ascended into heaven, and is seated at the right hand of God the Father almighty; from there he will come to judge the living and the dead.

I believe in the Holy Spirit, the holy catholic Church, the communion of saints, the forgiveness of sins, the resurrection of the body, and life everlasting. Amen.

## OUR FATHER

Our Father, who art in heaven, hallowed be thy name; thy kingdom come; thy will be done on earth as it is in heaven. Give us this day our daily bread; and forgive us our trespasses as we forgive those who trespass against us; and lead us not into temptation, but deliver us from evil. Amen.

## HAIL MARY

Hail Mary, full of grace, the Lord is with you;
blessed are you among women,
and blessed is the fruit of your womb, Jesus.
Holy Mary, Mother of God, pray for us sinners
now and at the hour of our death. Amen.

## GLORY BE

Glory be to the Father, the Son, and the Holy Spirit; as it was in the beginning, is now, and ever shall be, world without end. Amen.

## FATIMA PRAYER

O my Jesus, forgive us our sins, save us from the fires of hell, and lead all souls to heaven, especially those in most need of thy mercy.

# The Joyful Mysteries

*(Monday and Saturday)*

The Joyful Mysteries are exactly what they sound like — moments in the lives of Mary and Jesus that were full of great joy. As we ponder these events, let's especially ask God to help us see where he is filling our lives with his joy.

### THE JOYFUL MYSTERIES

The Annunciation
The Visitation
The Nativity
The Presentation
The Finding in the Temple

THE FIRST JOYFUL MYSTERY

# The Annunciation

The angel Gabriel appeared to Mary and announced that God had chosen her to be the mother of his Son. But because God created humans with free will, it meant that Mary could choose to say yes or no to God's plan to give the world a Savior.

In that moment, Mary had to decide whether or not to follow God's will. Even though she didn't know all the details and it meant letting go of her own plans, Mary trusted God.

In that moment, Mary knew the joy of saying yes to God and cooperating with his plan for her life.

✝

*Do you know and trust God enough to follow his plan for you like Mary did?*

*What are some things that God might be asking you to say yes to?*

THE SECOND JOYFUL MYSTERY

# The Visitation

When Mary heard from the angel Gabriel that her cousin Elizabeth was also pregnant, she immediately set out on a journey to be with her. Mary knew that the Good News that God was coming into the world was meant to be shared, and she wanted to bring it to those she loved.

Elizabeth was already happy because she was going to have a baby in her old age. But when Mary arrived, bringing Jesus in her womb, Elizabeth wasn't mad that Mary's miracle was bigger than hers. She was thrilled! Mary's joy didn't take away from Elizabeth's — it increased it.

It's a gift to be able to share our blessings with the people that we love and a gift to be able to rejoice in the miracles and blessings in their lives.

✝

*What are some of your blessings? Who can you share them with?*

*How do you respond when other people share their blessings with you?*

## THE THIRD JOYFUL MYSTERY

# The Nativity

The birth of Jesus probably didn't happen the way Mary thought it would. She was probably hoping to be home and surrounded by family and friends, not huddled in a stable surrounded by strangers and animals. Yet, that was the will of God. As Mary held in her arms the living, breathing Son of God incarnate, can you imagine that she had any thoughts to spare for what might have been? Who could want more than Jesus?

Mary was able to accept the unexpected way her son was born because she focused on him and not on anything else. Her focus on Jesus allowed her to experience the joy and wonder of Christ's birth.

†

*Have you ever been able to let go of your expectations and experience the joy of something different?*

*Have you ever had a hard time letting go of your expectations? Why?*

THE FOURTH JOYFUL MYSTERY

# The Presentation

When Jesus was 40 days old, Joseph and Mary took him to the Temple in Jerusalem to dedicate him to God. There they met an old man named Simeon who had been waiting his entire life for the Messiah. Simeon longed for him, prayed for him, and hoped for him so much that God had promised that he would not die without seeing the Savior promised to Israel.

And then there he was! Not only did Simeon get to see the Messiah, he got to hold him! As he cradled Jesus, Simeon rejoiced. Most people thought the Messiah would be a king or a warrior. But Simeon was able to recognize the baby Jesus as the Savior because of his deep relationship with God.

✝

*What are some ways that you can increase your closeness with God?*

*How do you think it felt for Simeon to experience the fulfillment of his dreams?*

THE FIFTH JOYFUL MYSTERY

# The Finding in the Temple

Mary and Joseph had taken Jesus on a trip to Jerusalem along with many other families. When they left to go home to Nazareth, they thought Jesus was walking with friends or neighbors. They didn't realize he had stayed behind. When they stopped for the night and realized that he was missing, they were scared and worried and hastily turned around to look for him.

Their fear turned into joy, when they found him after three days, safe and sound, teaching in the Temple. Mary and Joseph were grateful to have him back but didn't understand why he had stayed behind. Jesus reminded them that he needed to do the Father's will and helped them to see that God's plans are not always the same as those of ordinary people.

†

*Sometimes God turns our fears into joy too. Are there things in your life that you had been afraid of but later realized were wonderful?*

*Is there anything you are afraid of? How can you bring that to Jesus?*

# The Luminous Mysteries

*(Thursday)*

The Luminous Mysteries are the newest addition to the Rosary and were added by Pope St. John Paul II in 2002. Also known as the Mysteries of Light, these five moments in the life of Jesus shine light on his divinity. They give us glimpses into who Jesus is as the second Person of the Trinity. As we pray through these mysteries, let's especially ask God to help us see him in our everyday lives.

## THE LUMINOUS MYSTERIES

The Baptism in the Jordan
The Wedding Feast at Cana
The Proclamation of the Kingdom
The Transfiguration
The Institution of the Eucharist

THE FIRST LUMINOUS MYSTERY

# The Baptism in the Jordan

When he was ready to begin his public ministry, Jesus traveled from Nazareth to the Jordan River to be baptized by John the Baptist. John was Jesus' cousin, and he knew that Jesus was the Messiah. He knew that Jesus was sinless and that he, John, should be the one asking for baptism instead.

But Jesus knew God's plan. He knew that God wanted all people to be baptized and forgiven of their original sin and that he needed to show them how. So he insisted and was baptized.

When Jesus came out of the water, the heavens parted and the Holy Spirit came down like a dove. A voice from heaven said, "This is my beloved Son, with whom I am well-pleased."

✝

*What does this mystery tell us about who Jesus is? Why is that important?*

*What do you think the people by the riverbank felt when they heard the voice from heaven?*

THE SECOND LUMINOUS MYSTERY

# The Wedding Feast at Cana

One day Jesus and his mother went to a wedding together. During the celebration, Mary noticed that the couple had run out of wine for the guests to drink. She knew this would be embarrassing and asked Jesus to solve the problem so that the festivities could continue. Even when Jesus replied to her that his time to perform miracles hadn't arrived yet, Mary knew her son would help. She told the servants to do whatever Jesus told them to do, and sure enough he asked them to fill six stone jars full of water, draw some out, and bring it to the headwaiter. To everyone's surprise, the water had turned into excellent wine.

This was Jesus' first public miracle.

✝

*How do you think that Mary knew Jesus would act even when he told her no at first?*

*What does this miracle teach us about who Jesus is?*

THE THIRD LUMINOUS MYSTERY

# The Proclamation of the Kingdom

For three years Jesus traveled to town after town. Everywhere he went he taught people about God's love and mercy through his words and his actions.

He spoke in parables to help them understand that he was the Messiah, the Savior, God-Incarnate who had come to love them and bring them back to him.

He acted boldly and with love — healing the sick, welcoming the people who were most often left out or avoided, and forgiving sins.

Most of the time people didn't understand what Jesus was trying to show them. But some of the people who encountered Jesus believed. They left everything behind and followed him, becoming his disciples.

✝

*How do you think you would have reacted to Jesus if you heard him preaching and saw him working miracles?*

*Do you see Jesus working and speaking today? Where?*

THE FOURTH LUMINOUS MYSTERY

# The Transfiguration

Jesus took three of his apostles, Peter, James, and John, up a mountain to pray. As Jesus stood before them, his face shone like the sun and his clothes became dazzling white. Suddenly, Moses and Elijah, two of the most important prophets in Jewish history, appeared next to Jesus and began talking with him. Next, a bright cloud overshadowed them all and a voice spoke from the cloud saying, "This is my Beloved Son. Listen to him."

The three apostles became afraid and threw themselves on the ground, covering their faces. But Jesus came and gently touched them, telling them they didn't have to be afraid. And when they looked up, they saw only him.

†

*What do you think the three apostles were expecting when Jesus took them up the mountain?*

*If you were in their place, how would you have reacted to the vision? How do you think it changed their relationship with Jesus after?*

THE FIFTH LUMINOUS MYSTERY

# The Institution of the Eucharist

On the night before his death, Jesus gathered his twelve apostles together in an upper room to share something special with them. While they were sitting around the table, Jesus broke bread, blessed it, and held it up, telling them, "This is my Body, broken for you." And the bread had indeed become his Body. He did the same with the wine, changing it into his Precious Blood.

This sacred moment was the first Celebration of the Eucharist, but it would not be the last. At the Last Supper, Jesus gave the apostles the power to change bread and wine into his Body and Blood so that every generation to come could have Jesus fully present to them in the Eucharist.

†

*How do you think the apostles felt when they realized what Jesus was doing?*

*Do you let the gift of the Eucharist fill you with wonder?*

# The Sorrowful Mysteries

*(Tuesday and Friday)*

The Sorrowful Mysteries come from the Passion of Jesus. They are meant to remind us of what our Salvation cost Jesus (and Mary too because of her great love for him). They are meant to bring us to repentance for our own sins and gratitude for the Sacrifice of the Cross.

**THE SORROWFUL MYSTERIES**

The Agony in the Garden
The Scourging at the Pillar
The Crowning with Thorns
The Carrying of the Cross
The Crucifixion

THE FIRST SORROWFUL MYSTERY

# The Agony in the Garden

After the Last Supper, Jesus took his apostles into a garden to pray. He asked them to watch and pray, but even though they loved him, they fell asleep, leaving Jesus all alone. The apostles didn't know what was about to happen, but Jesus did. He was heartbroken and prayed so intensely that his sweat and tears were blood. But Jesus loved us more than he dreaded the thought of dying on the cross. So he ended his prayer by saying, "Father, not my will but yours be done."

✝

*How do you think that Jesus felt when his apostles fell asleep?*

*Have you ever felt alone? What helped you then?*

THE SECOND SORROWFUL MYSTERY

# The Scourging at the Pillar

After being arrested, Jesus was scourged. He was tied to a post and beaten with whips until his back was bleeding. But in this painful moment, he wasn't alone. Mary was there with him, watching in the crowd. Her presence gave him strength and comfort. Watching her precious son suffer must have felt almost impossible to Mary, but she loved him more than she wanted to avoid pain. Even though she couldn't do anything to stop it or protect him, she stayed.

†

*Has it ever helped you to have your mom with you in a tough moment?*

*Do you think you could have stayed with Jesus like Mary did and watched him suffer?*

## THE THIRD SORROWFUL MYSTERY

# The Crowning with Thorns

The soldiers wanted to make fun of Jesus and insult him. They brought him in front of a crowd of people, twisted thorn branches into a crown, and shoved it roughly onto his head. They put a robe on him and knelt in front of him, pretending to honor him as the King of the Jews.

†

*Jesus had come to die for the sins of the soldiers who were making fun of him. What do you think he felt when they were making fun of him?*

*What would you have felt if you were Mary witnessing the crowning with thorns?*

## THE FOURTH SORROWFUL MYSTERY

# The Carrying of the Cross

Criminals were made to carry their own crosses up to the hill where they would be hung on them. It was a long and painful journey, especially considering that Jesus had not slept or eaten and that he had just been beaten. The crowd pushed close on all sides — some people jeering, others weeping. Along the way, he saw the faces of those who loved him dearly like his mother Mary, John the Apostle, Mary Magdalene, and Veronica. They gave him comfort and strength. He also saw faces of those who hated him, but who he loved dearly anyway.

✝

*Jesus loved the people in the crowd even when they hated him. Do you believe that he loves you at your worst moments too?*

*If you were in the crowd and could speak to Jesus as he passed by, what would you say?*

## THE FIFTH SORROWFUL MYSTERY

# The Crucifixion

Jesus was nailed to the cross. His precious hands and feet were pierced with large nails. Being God, he could have saved himself. But he did not because his love for you was greater than the pain. Opening the gates of heaven, making it possible for all people to spend eternity with God, was more important to him than avoiding suffering. It was more important to Mary too. She stood at the foot of his cross offering him her love, support, and even agreeing to love all of us as a mother.

✝

*How do you feel when you think about Jesus being crucified?*

*As he hung on the cross, he forgave the people who put him there, which means he forgave us for our sins too. How does that make you feel?*

# The Glorious Mysteries

*(Wednesday and Sunday)*

The Glorious Mysteries are moments in the life of Jesus and Mary that show us God's splendor and majesty. They display the magnificence of God and remind us that heaven is waiting for us, and it is wonderful.

## THE GLORIOUS MYSTERIES

The Resurrection
The Ascension
The Descent of the Holy Spirit
The Assumption
The Coronation of Mary

THE FIRST GLORIOUS MYSTERY

# The Resurrection

Mary Magdalene went to Jesus' tomb to grieve. She was expecting to stand outside or perhaps kneel in front of the tomb and cry. She was not expecting an earthquake. She was not expecting an angel from heaven in all his brilliance. She was not expecting that angel to roll the stone away from Jesus' tomb revealing it to be empty.

And she was most certainly not expecting to hear Jesus' voice calling her name. In an instant, Mary's world was turned upside down. Her grief became joy. The world was different — Jesus was risen.

✝

*Have you ever experienced an unexpected reunion with someone you loved and thought you wouldn't get to see again? How did you feel?*

*What do you think Mary Magdalene was feeling at the tomb? How do you think you would have reacted to Jesus calling your name at that moment?*

THE SECOND GLORIOUS MYSTERY

# The Ascension

For forty days after the Resurrection, Jesus walked the earth again. He performed miracles. He reminded his apostles of what he had taught them. He made sure that they, along with his other disciples, knew how much he loved them.

But Jesus could not stay on earth forever. He needed to return to his Father in heaven. So he gathered his apostles to him one last time, and as they watched, he ascended into heaven and a cloud took him out of their sight.

✝

*What do you think it was like to be with Jesus after the resurrection?*

*How do you think Mary and the apostles felt when he ascended to heaven?*

THE THIRD GLORIOUS MYSTERY

# The Descent of the Holy Spirit

Jesus had told the apostles to wait in Jerusalem because he would send them the Holy Spirit to help and guide them. So they gathered with Mary in the same upper room where they had celebrated the Last Supper, praying and waiting for nine days. On the ninth day, the Holy Spirit appeared as tongues of fire and rested on their heads.

The Holy Spirit filled the apostles with wisdom and courage. They went out into the streets and began preaching the Gospel message publicly. From that day on, they traveled the world, speaking to everyone they met about Jesus, about his love for them, and about how he had died for their sins and rose again.

✝

*How do you feel about the idea of being filled with the Holy Spirit?*

*Mary had already been filled with the Holy Spirit at the Annunciation. What do you think she felt experiencing his coming and watching the apostles experience Pentecost?*

THE FOURTH GLORIOUS MYSTERY

# The Assumption of Mary

After Jesus' death, Mary lived with John the Apostle. He took care of her, and she took care of him. We don't know how long Mary lived, but we do know that it was likely for many more years. During those years, she encouraged and loved Jesus' apostles, and she provided strength for them in hard times. She prayed for them and for the new Church that was growing. But she was also waiting, waiting to see her son again. She had been separated from him in a way that she had never been before.

When Mary reached the end of her earthly life, because she was Immaculate and without sin, instead of dying and being buried, God chose to take her up into heaven both body and soul together. With the apostles surrounding her, Mary was assumed into heaven.

✝

*What do you think it was like for Mary to be without Jesus on earth?*

*What do you think Jesus said to Mary when they saw each other again for the first time after her assumption?*

## THE FIFTH GLORIOUS MYSTERY

# The Coronation of Mary

When Mary arrived in heaven, God crowned her as Queen of Heaven. She is queen because Jesus, her son, is King, but also because she worked with him to make our salvation possible by agreeing to be his mother.

Being a queen is a very high honor. Queens on earth have the power to rule, to make laws, to change the lives of their subjects for the better (or worse). As Queen of Heaven, Mary is also powerful, and she uses that power to help her children on earth by interceding for them. Just like he did on earth, Jesus listens to Mary. Just like she did on earth, Mary cooperates with God's will.

✝

*What do you think it was like in heaven when Mary was crowned queen?*

*What does it mean for your life that Mary, Queen of Heaven, is a mother to you?*

# Prayers after the Rosary

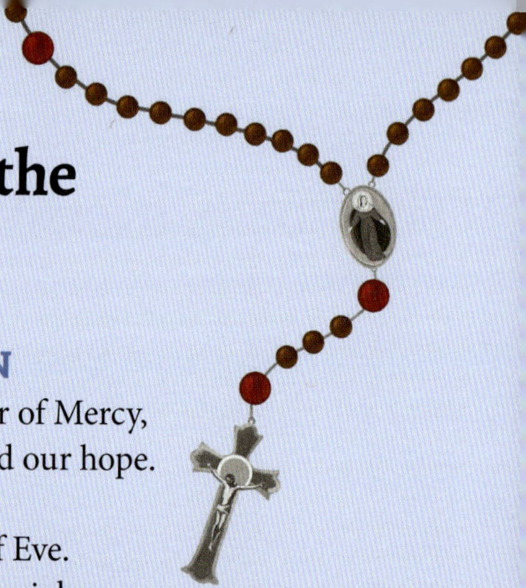

## HAIL, HOLY QUEEN

Hail, Holy Queen, Mother of Mercy,
our life, our sweetness and our hope.
To thee do we cry,
poor banished children of Eve.
To thee do we send up our sighs,
mourning and weeping in this valley of tears.
Turn then, most gracious advocate,
thine eyes of mercy toward us,
and after this our exile
show unto us the blessed fruit of thy womb, Jesus.
O clement, O loving,
O sweet Virgin Mary.

## CONCLUDING PRAYER

O God, whose only-begotten Son, by his life, death, and resurrection, has purchased for us the rewards of eternal life; grant, we beseech you, that we who meditate upon these mysteries of the most holy Rosary of the Blessed Virgin Mary, may imitate what they contain and obtain what they promise. We ask this through Christ our Lord. Amen.

## PRAYER TO ST. MICHAEL THE ARCHANGEL

St. Michael the Archangel, defend us in battle, be our protection against the wickedness and snares of the devil. May God rebuke him we humbly pray; and do thou, O Prince of the Heavenly Host, by the power of God, cast into hell Satan and all the evil spirits who prowl about the world seeking the ruin of souls. Amen.

## About the Author

A former missionary and former Montessori teacher, Colleen seeks to use the lessons she learned in the mission field and the classroom to live her dream of homeschooling and building the domestic church. Colleen lives with her husband, children, and grandmother in Michigan, where they enjoy everything about spring, summer, and fall, and hate the winters. She is the author of *Marian Consecration for Families with Young Children* (OSV, 2020), *Women Doctors of the Church* (OSV, 2022), and *The Jesse Tree for Families* (OSV, 2022).

## About the Illustrator

Steliyana Doneva is a children's book illustrator living in Sofia, Bulgaria. Her love of painting and drawing started in early childhood. Steliyana studied applied arts in Sofia, specializing in children's toys. She graduated with a degree in graphic arts, where she found her love for children's book illustration. Steliyana is very happy to be immersed in the beautiful fairy-tale world of illustrating children's books.

# More books from OSV Kids

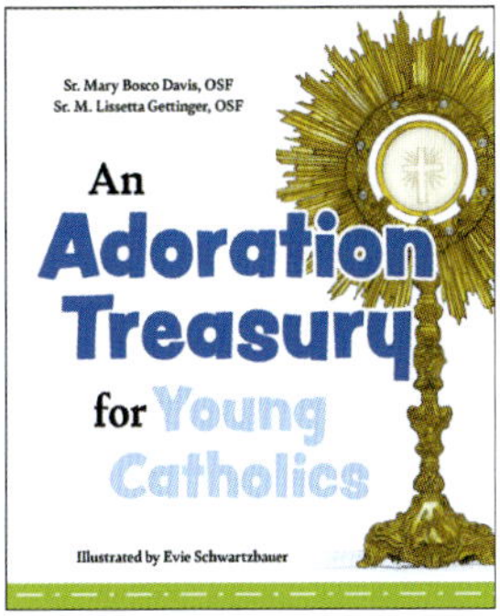


**An Adoration Treasury for Young Catholics**

*Sr. Mary Bosco Davis, OSF, and Sr. M. Lissetta Gettinger, OSF Illustrated by Evie Schwartzbauer*

In this adoration treasury, written by two Sisters of St. Francis of Perpetual Adoration — a religious order dedicated to perpetual adoration of Jesus in the Blessed Sacrament — young Catholics will find a multitude of prayers, hymns, meditations, and ways to pray before the Eucharist, accompanied by beautiful illustrations.

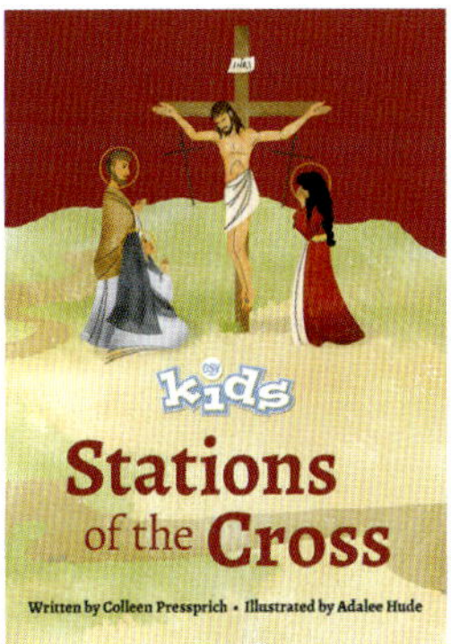


**OSV Kids Stations of the Cross**

*Written by Colleen Pressprich and illustrated by Adalee Hude*

OSV Kids Stations of the Cross helps children understand and connect with the Passion of Christ. Perfect for schools, parishes, and families, this wonderfully illustrated booklet includes age-appropriate descriptions of each Station, prayers, and questions for reflection and discussion.